GRANDMA'S KITCHEN

MORE FROM GRANDMA'S KITCHEN

COOKBOOK OF HOLIDAY AND EVERYDAY SOUL FOOD RECIPES

GRANDMA'S KITCHEN

TORNYNIA KINLAW

DALLAS, TEXAS

Copyright © 2021-2024 * Tornynia Kinlaw
Higgins Publishing | 1st Paperback Gift Edition, December 2024

All rights reserved. No part of this book may be reproduced or transmitted in any manner whatsoever without the written permission from the publisher, except in the case of brief quotations embodied in critical articles or reviews.

Library of Congress Cataloging in Publication Data

Names: Tornynia Kinlaw, Author
Title: GRANDMA'S KITCHEN:
Cookbook of Holiday and Everyday Soul Food Recipes
SBN 9781941580783 (Hardcover)
SBN 9781941580813 (Paperback)
Description: Dallas, TX: Tornynia Kinlaw 2024
Identifiers: LCCN 2024940980
p.c.m. 32

BISAC: CKB078000 COOKING / Regional & Cultural / Soul Food
BISAC: CKB042000 COOKING / Holiday
BISAC: CKB071000 COOKING / Reference

Our books may be purchased in bulk for promotional, educational, fundraising or business use. Please contact Higgins Publishing Sales Department at, sales@higginspublishing.com for ordering information.

Hardcover Manufactured in the United Kingdom

Published By:
Higgins Publishing
HigginsPublishing.com

EXECUTIVE EDITOR: Tiffany Knuckles
SENIOR EDITOR: Shanene Higgins

Editor's Note

GRANDMA's KITCHEN: *Cookbook of Holiday and Everyday Soul Food Recipes,* was inspired by my grandmother, her delicious food, and my passion for exploring the beautiful role that food plays in our lives.

I am not sure exactly where my love for food came from, but if I had to guess - it definitely has something to do with my grandmother and all the Sunday dinners and weekday meals she prepared for us. Her food brought our family together and I have some of my most fondest memories watching her cook and trying to help as best as my thirteen-year-old self could.

My grandmother's meals were some of the best meals I've had and I thought it essential to ensure that our family could recreate these dishes as a way of remembering and celebrating those moments together in Grandma's house.

I am so appreciative to my grandmother for sharing her recipes with me and for trusting me to carry on her traditions in the kitchen.

This book of recipes is dedicated back to my AMAZING grandmother Tornynia Kinlaw and to my beautiful niece, Charlee Knuckles.

All my love,

Tiffany Knuckles
Executive Editor

lineage
TABLE OF CONTENTS

06
Favorite Items
We asked Grandma what her favorite kitchen items and seasonings were. The items she shared are items she has to always have and couldn't imagine her kitchen without.

08
An Interview with Tornynia Kinlaw
Get to know Grandma as she shares her journey into how she became the cook she is today and how her family influenced her dishes.

11
Letter of Love
"Louder than Words" - by her middle daughter, Shanene.

recipes

WHAT RECIPES ARE IN THIS BOOK

14	Classic Macaroni & Cheese
15	Collard Greens
16	Pot Roast
17	Fresh Potato Salad
18	Thanksgiving Holiday Dressing
19	Sweet Potato Pie
20	Baked Beans
21	Stewed Cabbage
22	Pan Fried Pork Chop
23	Holiday Honey Baked Ham
24	Holiday Glazed Turkey
25	Southern Fried Chicken
26	Heavenly Cornbread

poetry
POEMS INSPIRED BY LEGACY

05

Grandma's Hands
A poem about the ancestral history, wisdom, and love that is shared through meals cooked by my grandmother.

12

Charlee
In April 2020, Charlee Mayse Knuckles was born. She is the first great-grandchild that my grandmother has and represents four generations of our family's bloodline.

27

Dedication
This final poem is a dedication to the person who inspired this book.

grandma's hands

BY TIFFANY KNUCKLES

Unwritten,
Tethered together by memories
and tastebuds that span more than three generations.
Shaped by time, pocketbooks,
and innovation
the essence still remains.

Down at the dinner table where
we meet.
Secrets and stories untold,
we bow our heads for grace,
mouths dry from anticipation
for what God has provided at the
fingertips of my grandmother's hands.

The salt lingers as the meat falls off
the bone
mixing with the richness of
the macaroni and cheese
the cornbread, straddling the sides

This was their intention.
God and my grandmother.
to tell the story of our ancestors
through hard earned
Sunday meals,
salt and pepper.
goodness and laughter.

Love in the form of overnight soaked
collard greens and hammocks.

We listen,
like children with wide imaginations
as she tells us what she's cooked today.

Our love for her mixed up in
"that-sounds-good" and
"I-need-that-recipe"
because sometimes "I love you"
doesn't roll off the tongue as well.

Like the taste of the plate
you saved for me
gently wrapped in foil stowed away
in the microwave.

May God bless the hands
that prepared this meal, we say.
As though from the start they were not.
But we know that
only blessed hands can create miracles.

Ancestral wisdom stirred into a pot,
behind a spoon.
Like a secret, only she knows.
we take more in with each bite.

LAWRY'S SEASONED SALT

Bring bold flavors to the table without spending hours in the kitchen. From baked chicken to deviled eggs, Lawry's gives all your meals that extra kick of flavor that you crave.

Ingredients include: Salt, Sugar, Spices (Including Paprika, Turmeric), Onion, Corn Starch, Garlic, and Sunflower Oil.

BUTTER

Butter is a dairy product made from the fat and protein components of milk or cream. It is used at room temperature as a spread, melted as a condiment, and used as an ingredient in baking, sauce making, pan frying, and other cooking procedures.

CINNAMON & NUTMEG

Cinnamon is from the bark of a tree, and nutmeg is a seed. Cinnamon is the "hot" flavor in a lot of candies, e.g. "Hot Tamales," as well as being used in apple pie and cinnamon rolls. Nutmeg is more subtle, often used with other spices, sometimes including cinnamon. Separately or together, cinnamon and nutmeg work magic in baking and desserts, heightening flavors and aromas.

CAST IRON SKILLET

Heavy-duty cookware made of cast iron is valued for its heat retention, durability, ability to be used at very high temperatures, and non-stick cooking when properly seasoned. Seasoning is also used to protect bare cast iron from rust.

DUTCH OVEN

A Dutch oven is a thick-walled cooking pot with a tight-fitting lid. Dutch ovens are usually made of seasoned cast iron; however, some Dutch ovens are instead made of cast aluminum, or ceramic. A Dutch oven is perfect for braises because of how heavy it is, which helps it retain and distribute heat evenly—ideal for searing meat at high heat and maintaining low-and-slow temperatures for a long time.

ROASTING PAN

A roasting pan is a piece of cookware used for roasting meat in an oven, either with or without vegetables or other ingredients. A roasting pan may be used with a rack that sits inside the pan and lets the meat sit above the fat and juice drippings. A roasting pan is an oven safe, high walled pan most commonly used to cook a large cut of meat, vegetables, and/or starches at a high temperature — usually 350 degrees and hotter.

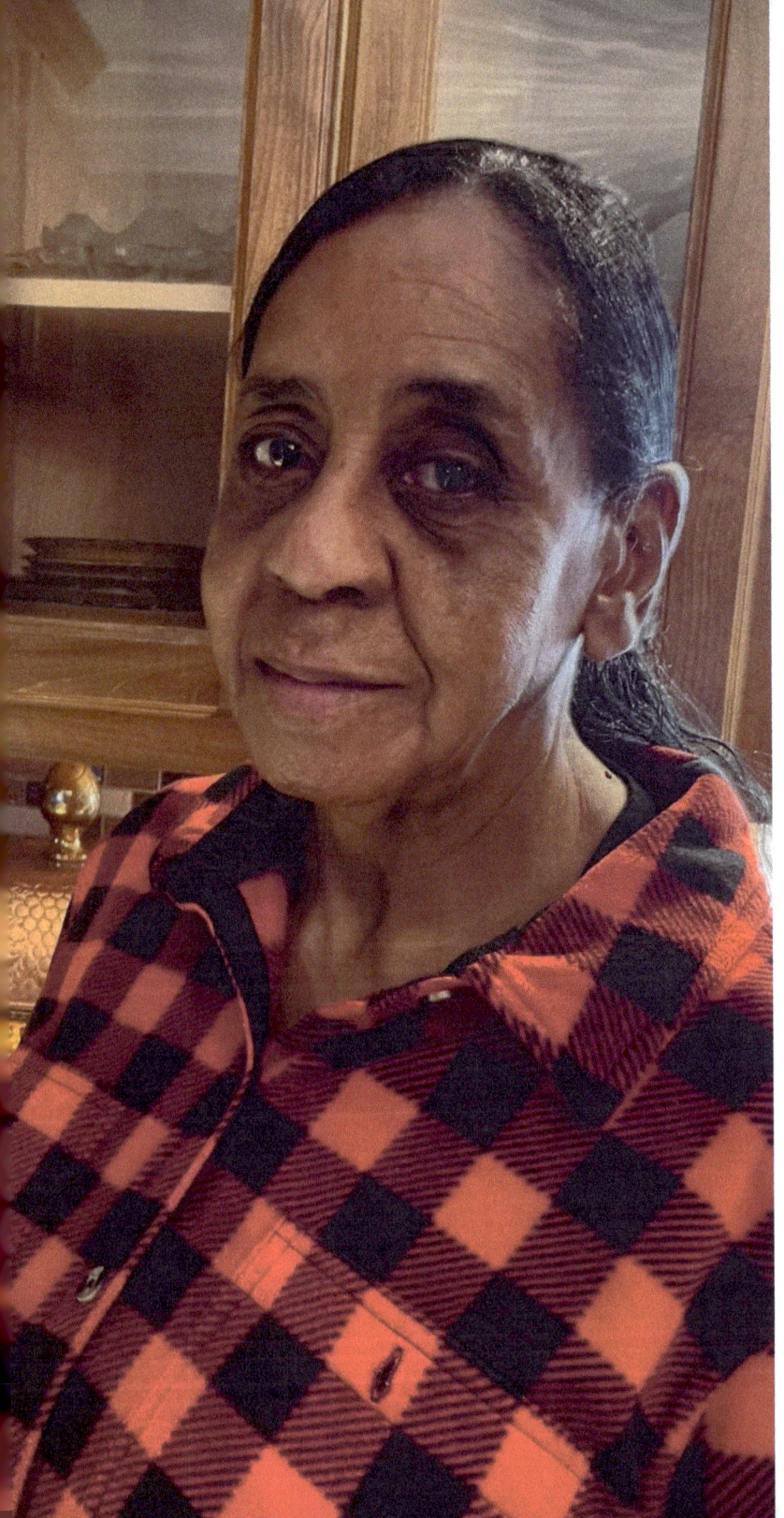

Interview with Tornynia Kinlaw

What is your first food memory?

My first food memory was when Deb showed me how to cook grits, liver, and biscuits. I was about 16 years old. She was one of the first people who showed me how to cook and ever since then I have been developing my own flavors based on what I like, and what my family likes to eat.

Has food or family meals been a part of your family tradition?

I started learning from the age of 16 and that started me on a path towards practicing different things. My mother and my brother cooked a lot. I remember, they cooked chicken and turkey during the holidays.

They cooked a lot of rice, popcorn bread, patties, neck bones and northern beans, gravy and rice, and smothered pork chops. I remember eating a lot of chicken, pork chops, hamburgers, mashed potatoes, rice and vegetables in our home.

My mother and brother would always eat cereal for breakfast, but for other meals, they usually made full meals. On holidays and on some birthdays, I would do a dinner with gumbo. Sometimes I would cook shrimp, cornbread, or bake a turkey, things like that. Food was always a part of our family tradition.

As you started your own family, how have you seen food bring your family together?

I would say that my family enjoyed food very much. My daughter, Shay would help me sometimes. She would chop the different ingredients and have different beverages to go with the meals...never liquor. All my cooking has been delicious. I had a couple of daughters that wanted to learn a couple of things. I showed my first daughter, Shay.

When did you first begin cooking and how did you develop your skills?

I got married, so it was around the time when I had to feed my husband as well as my kids. I just cooked a full meal, because that's what I was used to seeing. I was always raised around that type of cooking.

I started making chili. That was a favorite of Larry Foster, my partner at the time, so

that's what I started cooking for him. The more I cooked, the better I got. I continued making macaroni and cheese, collard greens and the types of foods I grew up with. For the most part, the recipes have always been the same and passed down from how I saw my mother and brother do it. Some small details might have changes, but the basics remain the same. For instance, with my cornbread, everyone says it tastes like cake. So I started making cornbread muffins... like little cupcakes.

Any particular items you made for other members of your family?

My grandson Douglas - he loved macaroni and cheese, so I would always fix him his own. He also really loved my cornbread. My daughter, Sunshine, has mastered my Mac and Cheese.

My granddaughter, Sierra and daughter Shanene, love my potato salad. I use Ms. Dash to make it especially for them. My granddaughters, Mia and Squeak love my baked beans! Shanene also says my dressing and potato salad should be in Costco!

❝ LOUDER THAN WORDS

You've always been someone to depend on.
Even when I was too proud to ask for help.
Regardless of what life threw your way
You always found a way to bless others
With your giving and loving heart.
Even though you don't always express
How you feel in words, your actions
speak louder than any words can say.
Thanks for always being an example
Of an unselfish giving person
Even when times were tough!

YOU ALWAYS FOUND A WAY TO BLESS OTHERS...

❞

You are an example of unwavering unconditional love and acceptance.

Happy 78th Birthday!

Love, Your Middle Child...
Shanene

charlee

BY TIFFANY KNUCKLES

Sun-kissed, she smiles a smile that extends for generations
Uttering her first words the first day she arrived
We knew the future would unfold for her
And with her at the center.

She is the extension of a tethered together
Sometimes dysfunctional always a family, family
Even when our calls become desperate over the terrain of miles
And the complacency of settling into our rhythms
Folds itself into nostalgia of the yesteryears,
She is the beginning again.

I wonder if in her genes remains the memories
of our many moments.
When we were all our best selves together.
On a cul-de-sac street of San Leandro
Second to the last house on the right, just before the setting sun,
And the smell of pot roast seeping into the foil,
and into streets.

Charlee, is the recipient of those memories.
All the uninterrupted laughs and mouths full of food.
That could not anticipate today
But somehow
In time, and in the exact moment we all needed her,
She came to be.

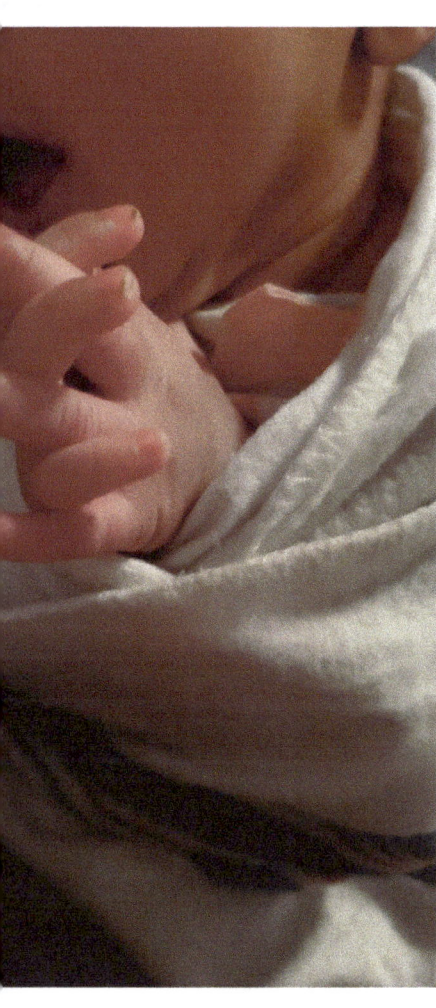  

Charlee Mayse

RECIPES

Classic Macaroni & Cheese

Yield: One 12-inch Pan of Mac & Cheese
Prep Time: 15 minutes
Total Time: 30-40 minutes
Temperature: 350 Degrees

Sometimes, you just can't beat a classic like a creamy and simple pan of Macaroni and Cheese. This homemade recipe hits the spot and is so easy to make!

INGREDIENTS

- 2 Slices of American Cheddar Cheese
- 1 Pack of Cheddar Cheese
- 1 Pack of Macaroni
- 1 Stick of Butter
- 1 Cup of Milk
- 1/2 Tbsp of Accent Seasoning
- Pinch of Seasoning Salt

PROCEDURE

1. Bring water to boil in medium sauce pan; add package of macaroni. Cook for 6-7 minutes until al dente. Drain and rinse macaroni.

2. Transfer to mixing bowl. Add cheese, butter, accent, seasoning salt and milk to macaroni.

3. Break butter into small pieces and place around oven-proof baking pan. Pour macaroni mixture into pan and add slices of cheese to the top.

4. Place oven proof dish into oven and bake macaroni uncovered for 30-40 minutes.

5. Remove from the oven and let stand before serving.

RECIPES

Collard Greens

Yield: 5 Quart Covered Stock Pot
Prep Time: 2 Hours
Cook Time: 4 Hours
Total Time: 6 Hours

Nothing says southern home cooked meal like a pot of greens. This timeless vegetable is a staple in many Black homes and is always a good reminder of our roots.

INGREDIENTS

- 6-8 Bunches of collard greens
- Seasoning salt
- 1 tbsp of Crisco
- 1 Ham hock
- 1/2 tbsp of vinegar
- 2 tbsp of tenderizer
- Accent (sprinkle to taste)

PROCEDURE

1. Thoroughly wash greens. Once washed, roll up each leaf like folding a burrito, then slice from end to end into small portions. Then rinse cut greens one final time.

2. Place greens in pot and cook on medium high temperature for 4 hours.

3. As greens cook, sprinkle with accent. Taste as needed.

4. While greens cook, cut up ham hock.

5. Add ham hock and crisco butter to pot and blend together.

6. Add a sprinkle of sugar to taste. Add water to greens as needed making sure greens are always covered with water.

7. Continuously check until greens are tender. Once cooked and fully tender, turn off heat and serve.

Pot Roast

Yield: One Oval Roasting Pan
Prep Time: 15 Minutes
Total Time: 1-2 Hours

With this roast, tenderizer goes a long way. Get a juicy pot roast every time and impress the whole family with this mouth watering protein.

INGREDIENTS

- 1 can golden mushroom soup
- 1 can cream of mushroom
- Tenderizer
- 1 Onion; chopped
- 2 Golden Potatoes; chopped
- 2 Cups Water

PROCEDURE

1. Set oven to 375 degrees.

2. Chop onions and Potatoes into quarters.

3. Season roast with tenderizer, from top to bottom.

4. Place roasting pan, onions, and potatoes in oven for 1-2 Hours; until tender.

5. Drain some of the water from the roast near the end of the second hour, then pour cream of mushroom soup and golden mushroom onto roast.

6. Continue to cook roast and add water as needed if roast seems dry.

7. Turn off heat and remove from oven. Let rest for 10 to 15 minutes before serving.

Fresh Potato Salad

Yield: One 12-14 Inch Casserole Dish
Prep Time: 10 Minutes
Cook Time: 30-40 Minutes
Total Time: 1 Hour

Potato salad can be served on a hot summer day at a family barbecue or as a side dish to any soul food dinner that needs a fresh and filling element.

INGREDIENTS

- 7 White Potatoes
- 5 Eggs; Boiled
- 3 Tbsp Mayo
- Grey Poupon Dijon Mustard
- 2 Tbsp Sweet Relish
- 1 Tbsp Sugar
- Salt and Pepper; to taste
- Top Paprika
- Green Onions (optional topping)

PROCEDURE

1. Bring pot of water to a boil, season with a sprinkle of salt.

2. Slowly add potatoes to hot water. Let cook for 45 minutes, or until potatoes are soft enough to pierce with a fork.

3. While potatoes are cooking, add eggs to same pot and cook for 10-15 minutes. Remove eggs from heat, let cool, and de-shell. Place to the side.

4. Remove potatoes from water, and let cool. Once cooled, peel each potato and cut into small blocks.

5. Once potatoes are cut, add mayo, relish, grey poupon. Once mixed, add sugar to mixed potato salad. Transfer mixture to serving bowl.

6. Slice eggs into several round circles. Top potato salad mixture with sliced egg rounds and sprinkle paprika lightly over the top.

7. Refrigerate for at least 1 hour before serving.

Thanksgiving Holiday Dressing

Yield: 1 Cast Iron Pan
Prep Time: 10 Min
Cook Time: 30 Min
Total Time: 40 Min

Thanksgiving is a time where the whole family comes together. Be sure to make this dressing (sometimes called stuffing) to accompany your holiday meal.

INGREDIENTS

- 1 Pack gizzards
- 1 Bell Pepper, diced
- 1/2 can of cream of mushroom soup
- 1/2 Bag of Croutons
- 4 Eggs
- Crisco Butter
- Pinch of Salt
- Poultry Seasoning
- Sage

PROCEDURE

1. Use cornbread recipe to make a pan of cornbread.

2. Cook gizzards in pot of water seasoned with sage, and poultry seasoning.

3. In a large bowl, break cooked cornbread up into small pieces.

4. Dice bell peppers finely. Saute bell peppers in tbsp of Crisco butter. Add cooked bell peppers to cornbread mixture. Season with pinch of salt.

5. Add cooked gizzards to mixture.

6. Add in the cream of mushroom soup, and the egg then fold the ingredients all together.

7. Grease a pan with Crisco butter. Pour dressing mixture into pan. Let back, covered, for 1 hour. Then finish baking, uncovered for 30 minutes.

8. Turn off heat and remove from oven. Let rest for 10 to 15 minutes before serving.

RECIPES

Sweet Potato Pie

Yield: 4-6 Pies (Serve in Baking Pans)
Prep Time: 20 Minutes
Total Time: 1 Hour
Temperature: 350 Degrees

Talk about a dessert for the soul! Enjoy a slice (or two) of sweet potato pie hot or room temperature after a hearty meal. You can't go wrong with a nice crumbly crust and smooth center.

INGREDIENTS

- 8 Yams/Sweet Potatoes
- 1 Stick of Butter
- 1 Can of Cream
- 1 Pre-Made Pie Crust
- 1/2 Tbsp of Cinnamon
- 1/2 Tbsp of Nutmeg
- Sugar, to taste

PROCEDURE

1. Boil sweet potatoes for 20-30 Minutes or until able to pierce with fork. Remove potatoes from water, and let cool.

2. Preheat oven to 350 Degrees.

3. Peel potatoes then mix with butter, cream, cinnamon, nutmeg, and sugar (to taste).

4. Dust each backing pan/pre-made pie crust with flour. Transfer mixture to baking pans until all pans are filled.

5. Place several pies in the oven at one time. Bake for 15-20 minutes or until pies are slightly browned.

RECIPES

Baked Beans

Yield: 4-6 Pies (Serve in Baking Pans)
Prep Time: 10 Minutes
Total Time: 30 Minutes
Temperature: 375 Degrees

These sweet baked beans will be like no other baked beans you've ever had. So good they'll make you want to slap your momma. Don't do that, but you understand...

INGREDIENTS

- 1 Large Can of Baked Beans
- 1/2 Stick of Butter
- 1/2 Cup of Organic Sugar
- 1 Tbsp Cinnamon
- 1 Tbsp Nutmeg
- 1/2 Cup of Mrs. Butterworth Syrup

PROCEDURE

1. Pour can of beans into mixing bowl.

2. Add butter, sugar, cinnamon, nutmeg, and syrup to beans and mix well.

3. Place bean mixture into baking pan and cook for approximately 40 minutes.

4. Remove from oven, and let cool a bit before serving.

RECIPES

Stewed Cabbage

Yield: One Pot of Cabbage
Prep Time: 15 Min
Cook Time: 2 hr 15 Min
Total Time: 2 hr 30 min

Cabbage is a hearty vegetable served in many homes in the most southern households. This recipe includes the use of crisco butter, a family favorite.

INGREDIENTS

- 1 Cabbage
- 1 Ham Hock
- 1 Chopped Onion
- Salt and Pepper to taste
- Crisco Butter
- Accent/Tenderizer

PROCEDURE

1. Wash then cut a head of cabbage into small sections.

2. Place ham hock in small pot with tenderizer. Fill pot with water and cook ham hock for 2 hours on medium heat.

3. Add cabbage and chopped onions to second medium size pot. Season with tenderizer, accent, a small amount of salt and pepper. Cook on medium heat.

4. Once ham hock is cooked with tenderizer, drain water, cut ham hock into pieces and put into pot with cabbage.

5. Add small amount of butter and cook down slowly.

6. Let flavors blend and serve after approximately 20 minutes.

RECIPES

Pan Fried Pork Chop

Prep Time: 10 Minutes
Cook Time: 20 Minutes
Total Time: 30 Minutes

Say goodbye to dry and flavorless pork chops. With a few simple tricks, you can make juicy and tender pork chops in just a few easy steps.

INGREDIENTS

- 1 package of pork chops
- Tenderizer
- Pepper
- Crisco Butter
- Oil
- Flour

PREP TIME: 10 Minutes
COOK TIME: 20 Minutes
TOTAL TIME: 30 Minutes

PROCEDURE

1. Wash pork chops with water then pat dry and set on cutting board.

2. Use fork to slightly pierce pork chops on both sides to tenderize the meat.

3. Season pork chops with tenderizer, pepper, and other seasonings to your preference.

4. Lightly flour each pork chop to create a nice batter around the entire chop.

5. Heat your skillet to medium and drizzle oil into skillet.

6. Place pork chops into hot skillet and brown on both sides to your satisfaction.

7. Once cooked, placed chops on a plate to the side and cover with foil until ready to serve.

RECIPES

Holiday Honey Baked Ham

Yield: One Roasting Pan
Prep Time: 10 min
Cook Time: 60 Min - 90 Min
Total Time: 1hr+
Temperature: 375 Degrees

Ham is an excellent highlight for any large gathering or holiday meal. For many, nothing is better during the holidays than a delicious ham baking in the oven.

INGREDIENTS

- Ham
- Cherries
- Brown Sugar
- 1 Can of Pineapple Juice
- Toothpicks
- Foil

PROCEDURE

1. Wash ham.

2. Place cherries over ham with toothpicks.

3. In a bowl, mix brown sugar with pineapple juice (or water and flour mix) and prepare to pour over ham.

4. Line roasting pan with foil so ham doesn't stick to the pan.

5. Place ham in roasting pan and rub brown sugar mix all over ham.

5. Cook for 60 to 90 minutes at 375 degrees and remove from oven.

RECIPES

Holiday Glazed Turkey

Yield: 1 Large Roasting Pan
Prep Time: 30 Minutes
Cook Time: 4-6 Hours
Total Time: 4-6 Hours
Temperature: 375 Degrees

Turkey is often the centerpiece of the Thanksgiving table, so you want to have an impressive recipe in your back pocket. Get ready to show off your skills with this family recipe!

INGREDIENTS

- Ms. Butterworth Turkey
- 1 container/pack of turkey gizzard
- Butter
- Turkey bag (if desired)
- Tenderizer
- Salt and pepper, to taste

PROCEDURE

1. Unpack the turkey and remove all ingredients from inside of it (neck, gizzards, unnecessary guts, etc.) Clean the inside as best as possible. (You can cook neck and gizzards separately). Preheat oven to 375 degrees.

2. Wash the turkey completely - inside and out. Then season all over with tenderizer.

3. Place seasoned turkey into roasting pan, and glaze it with butter. You can either place turkey in turkey bag or simply cover roasting pan with aluminum foil.

4. Check turkey every hour to prevent overcooking and/or burning.

5. Once the turkey has almost cooked, add dressing to the inside of the turkey and allow the turkey to continue cooking until done.

RECIPES

Southern Fried Chicken

Prep Time: 10 Minutes
Cook Time: 20 Minutes
Total Time: 30 Minutes

Say goodbye to dry flavorless chicken! With a few simple tricks you can make juicy and tender chicken in just a few easy steps.

INGREDIENTS

- 1 Package of Chicken
- Tenderizer
- Pepper
- Crisco Butter
- Canola Oil
- Flour

PROCEDURE

1. Wash each piece of the chicken and then dry and set on a cutting board.

2. Use a fork to slightly pierce each piece on both sides to tenderize the chicken.

3. Season the chicken with tenderizer, pepper and other seasonings of choice.

4. Lightly flour each piece to create a batter over the entire piece of chicken.

5. Heat your skillet to medium and drizzle oil and Crisco Butter into the skillet.

6. Place each piece into hot skillet and brown on both sides to your satisfaction. Once cooked, place each piece of chicken in a serving dish, and cover until ready to serve.

RECIPES

Heavenly Cornbread

Yield: 1 Cast Iron Skillet
Prep Time: 10 Minutes
Bake Time: 20-30 Minutes
Total Time: 40 Minutes

Nothing says southern down home cooking like warm, buttery, fluffy corn bread. This simple recipe can be added to any soul food dish!

INGREDIENTS

- 2 cups of Flour
- 1.5 cups of Corn Meal
- 1 Cup of Milk
- 1 Egg
- 2 Tbsp of Sugar
- 1 Tbsp of Baking Powder
- 1/2 Stick of Butter
- 1 Pinch of Salt
- 1 Spoon Crisco Butter (melted)

PROCEDURE

1. Preheat oven to 350 degrees.

2. Place each item into a large bowl and mix all ingredients.

3. Once combined, stir until no lumps are visible.

4. Grease your skillet and then pour cornbread mixture into skillet.

5. Place skillet in the oven and bake for 20-30 Minutes.

6. Test doneness of cornbread by sticking a butter knife in the center. If you are able to lift the knife with no cornbread residue, pull your skillet from the oven.

7. Butter the top of your cornbread and prepare to serve.

dedication

BY TIFFANY KNUCKLES

I hope she knows
this is for her.
For all the missed calls and sweetly asked favors
For the years of not talking
and the years of talking too much

For trusting me behind the wheel
and showing me the way

For all the truth-telling and
early morning prayers
I never knew were said for me

For all the scratcher earned cash
that put food on the table

For all the washed dishes
and swept up floors

For all the strength we have that came from her
That passed through my mother's belly
and into me, into my bones.
Infused into my DNA
Infused into the marrow of our memories

For all the things and everything in between

If you enjoy this cookbook, please post a review where you purchased **GRANDMA'S KITCHEN.**

Thank you.

www.ingramcontent.com/pod-product-compliance
Lightning Source LLC
Chambersburg PA
CBHW040006080526
44586CB00027B/2897